<small>A
Little</small> Middle East Cookbook

Jacquey Visick

ILLUSTRATED BY KATHERINE GREENWOOD

Chronicle Books

First published in 1993 by
The Appletree Press Ltd,
19–21 Alfred Street, Belfast BT2 8DL
Tel. +44 232 243074 Fax +44 232 246756

A Little Middle Eastern Cookbook

First published in the United States in 1993 by
Chronicle Books, 275 Fifth Street,
San Francisco, CA 94103

ISBN: 0-8118-0339-2

9 8 7 6 5 4 3 2 1

Introduction

Just where does the Middle East begin and end? Borders are changing. So are our ideas. Today's "new" Europe includes the old Near East – the Balkan States – and stretches as far as the former Soviet states of Georgia, Armenia, and Azerbaidzhan. Yet those three, with their backs to the Caucasus Mountains, are linked to a "culinary" Middle East that spans the Yemen in the south and the Black Sea shores of Turkey in the north, Iran in the east and Egypt in the west, and saunters on through the Mahgreb, those North African lands lapped by the Mediterranean Sea, as far as Morocco. What unites them all are the over-lapping influences of the Arab, Islamic, and Ottoman empires.

One of the joys of recreating this aromatic and delicately-spiced food is to explore specialty stores – Greek, Turkish, Lebanese, Iranian – making new discoveries, or buying something as familiar as mint from people who take fresh herbs so seriously that they sell them in bunches big enough for a flower arrange-ment but at a fraction of the cost. Do read each recipe through before you shop and before you start cooking. They are all tried and tested but don't hesitate to experiment and adapt. Cook with your taste buds. And do what Middle Eastern cooks do: use what is available.

A note on measures
Spoon measurements are level except where otherwise indi-cated. Seasonings can of course be adjusted according to taste. Recipes are for four unless otherwise indicated.

Hummus

Chick-pea Purée

Hummus, el-ful, falafel, tabbouleh, dolmades, and tahina cream paste, are all part of the myriad of delectable Arab and Mediterranean appetizers known collectively as *mezzeh*. For a complete summer meal, serve all six with dishes of olives, salted nuts, cherry tomatoes and sticks of salted cucumber. "Eat of the good things that God has granted": Koran, Chapter VII, verse 160.

---

1 cup chick-peas
juice of 2 lemons
1/2 cup ready-made, sesame-based, tahini paste
3–4 large cloves garlic
salt and pepper
olive oil
parsley

Soak the chick-peas overnight. Drain them. Put them in a heavy pan with plenty of unsalted water. Bring to a boil and simmer until tender – about one hour – removing any scum. Keep the cooking liquid when you drain them. Combine the chick-peas, lemon juice, tahini paste, crushed garlic, and a little cooking liquid in a food processor. As you blend it, add enough oil and cooking liquid to create a thick and slightly granular paste. Add salt and pepper to taste. Sprinkle the hummus with a handful of finely chopped parsley. Serve with pitta bread (see p. 16).

El-ful or Ful Medames

Egyptian Brown Beans

The nobility of dynastic Egypt ate well. Cheese, wine, stewed figs, beer, fish, pigeon, quail, and wheaten bread were all found in a tomb of the third millennium B.C. Yet ask an Egyptian today, rich or poor, to name his or her favorite food, and many will name the humblest of dishes: *el-ful*.

2 cups dried ful medames or	parsley, finely chopped
fava beans	salt to taste
6 eggs	olive oil
4 cloves crushed garlic	parsley, finely chopped
3 tbsp olive oil	garlic
1 tbsp ground cumin	turmeric or paprika

Soak the beans overnight. Drain them. Put them in a large, sturdy pan with water, eggs (in their shells), crushed garlic, oil, and cumin. Bring to a boil, cover, and simmer very gently until the beans are *just* soft, but not overcooked (approximately 2 hours). If you take out the eggs after the first 20–30 minutes, crack the shells very gently, then return them still in the shell to continue cooking, the whites should become attractively "marbled". Drain the beans and put them in a bowl, adding the following ingredients according to taste: salt, olive oil, lemon juice, finely chopped parsley, and garlic. Stir them thoroughly. Crown the beans with the shelled eggs and sprinkle with turmeric or paprika.

Falafel or Ta'amia

Chick-pea Rissoles

Falafel is the Israeli name and *ta'amia*, or *tameya*, the Coptic. The Copts – descendants of the ancient Egyptians – claim this dish as their own and it may well have been eaten by the Pharaohs. Certainly the Sumerians were growing chick-peas in Babylonia in the fourth millennium B.C. and left cultivation notes in one of the world's earliest surviving reference works, the Sumerian "Farmers' Almanac" of about 2,500 B.C.

---

1 cup dried chick-peas, soaked overnight
2 cloves crushed garlic
2 mild, medium-size onions, very finely chopped
1 bunch parsley, finely chopped
1 tsp each ground coriander and cumin
¹/₂ tsp each turmeric and baking powder
¹/₄ tsp cayenne
salt and black pepper to taste
vegetable oil for frying
seasoned flour

Drain the chick-peas. In a medium saucepan cover them in fresh unsalted water and simmer until soft (about one hour). Combine all the ingredients (except the oil) in a food pro-cessor, but quickly, so that the mixture still has texture, but is sufficiently sticky to bind when rolled by hand. Let it rest for half an hour. Then roll walnut-size shapes and coat them in seasoned flour. Either deep fry them or fry them in a shallow pan, moving them about so they become golden. Drain them on paper towels. Serve cold with Tahina Cream Sauce (see p. 15).

Tabbouleh

Cracked Wheat Salad

Burghul is the Arab name for cracked wheat, *bulgar* the Turkish, and *pourgouri* the Greek. The whole wheat grains are parboiled, dried in the sun, and then ground. There is no such thing as a definitive Middle Eastern *tabbouleh* recipe. The essential flavor comes from lemon juice and fresh parsley. Don't stint on either.

---

1 cup cracked wheat known as burghul, bulgar *or* pourgouri
2–3 tbsp finely chopped spring onion, or onion
4 tomatoes, finely chopped
¹/₂ cucumber, peeled and finely chopped
4–6 rounded tbsp parsley, finely chopped
3 tbsp finely chopped fresh mint, or 2 of dried mint
juice of 2–3 lemons (or more, to taste)
4 tbsp olive oil
salt and black pepper to taste
lettuce or vine leaves and black olives to garnish

Soak the wheat in plenty of water for 45 minutes. It will swell a great deal. Drain it, pressing out all the excess water. The drier it is, the more it can take up the other flavors. Put the wheat in a large bowl. Gently stir in all the other ingredients, except the garnishes, maintaining the characteristically lemon-and-parsley flavor. Arrange the lettuce or vine leaves around a serving bowl or dish and heap the *bulgar* in the center. Decorate it with black olives, or wedges of tomato, or lemon.

Dolmades

Stuffed Vine Leaves

Dolaman is the Turkish word for a garment or anything else that wraps-around. *Dolma* or *dolmades* means any vegetable, including the vine leaf, wrapped around a filling. This version can be eaten cold.

---

packet of vine leaves (or fresh young vine leaves)
1 1/4 cups uncooked long grain rice
4 tbsp spring onion, finely chopped
2 tomatoes, skinned and chopped
2 tbsp each dried chopped mint and
finely chopped fresh parsley
pinch of cinnamon, pinch of allspice
1/2 cup olive oil
salt, pepper, sugar, and the juice of 1 lemon
(makes 24–30)

Soak the vine leaves in boiling water. Drain and rinse them when cool. Trim away the stems. Use coarse and damaged leaves to line a large pan. Pour boiling water over the rice. Let it soak for 10 minutes. Drain and rinse under running cold water, and drain it again. Put rice in a bowl with the tomatoes, spring onion, herbs, spices, salt, and pepper. Mix thoroughly. Place a teaspoonful of the mixture on the base of each leaf and roll into a small parcel, tucking in the sides. Pack the *dolmades* tightly into the pan. Pour in the olive oil and lemon juice, add a teaspoon of sugar and enough water to cover them. Bring to boiling point, reduce the heat, and simmer gently for about 2 hours, topping up the liquid. Cool in the pan and serve warm or cold.

Sauces

Tahina Cream Sauce

Tahina paste, made from toasted, ground sesame seeds, is readily available from Greek stores. Stir it well before use. Serve the sauce as a starter with Arab bread and as an accompaniment to main dishes such as *Samakah Harrah* (see p. 39).

2–3 cloves garlic, minimum	juice of 2 lemons
¹/₂ cup tahini paste	1 tsp salt
¹/₂ cup plain yogurt or water	

Blend the garlic and salt together. Add the tahina paste, then the yogurt or water and lastly the lemon juice.

Bazha: Walnut Sauce

Eating habits in some parts of the Middle East are necessarily frugal because of the climate. In Georgia there is an abundance of produce, and hospitality achieves epic proportions. Walnut sauce is a specialty of the central region of Kartli.

1 cup shelled walnuts	3 tbsp fresh coriander,
1–6 cloves garlic	or mint, or parsley
¹/₄ cup wine vinegar	salt and cayenne pepper
¹/₂ cup water	to taste
¹/₄ cup spring onions	

Combine all the ingredients in a blender. Taste for seasoning. Delicious as a dip for meatballs, or for sliced eggplant, fried in oil and served cold.

Pitta Bread

The classic Arab bread is made without oil. The addition of oil makes it softer and quite delicious. It miraculously creates its own pouch.

---

4 cups all-purpose flour
1 tsp salt
pinch of sugar
2 tbsp oil
1/4 oz dried yeast
1 1/4 cups lukewarm water
(makes 8)

Sift the salt and flour into a bowl. Dissolve the sugar in half the water, add the yeast and stir. Leave in a warm place until frothy. Make a well in the flour. Add the yeast mixture and the oil. Mix by hand, adding the remaining water. Knead until the dough is soft and slightly sticky. Continue to knead on a floured surface until it is elastic and silky – about 15–20 minutes. Shape into a ball and put it into an oiled bowl, coating the entire surface of the dough. Cover the bowl with plastic wrap. Leave in a warm place until the dough doubles in bulk (about 2 hours). Knead it for another 5 minutes. Divide into 8 pieces and roll them out on a floured surface until they are about a quarter inch thick. Rest them for half an hour in the warmth, covered with a cloth. Heat the oven to its maximum. Oil the baking trays and put them in the hot oven for 10 minutes. Slide the breads onto them and cook for 6–8 minutes. The pitta will swell up, creating the internal pouch. Cool on wire racks.

Khubz-el-Saluf

Fenugreek and Coriander Pitta Bread

This pitta bread is found all along the southern coast of the Arabian peninsula, from Muscat to Yemen. The proximity of the Indian subcontinent has had a fiery influence on the cooking of this area. Start by soaking 1/4 cup of fenugreek seeds (which don't look like seeds) in water overnight (no longer, or they will sprout). Next day, prepare the dough according to the recipe for pitta bread on page 16. While the rolled-out pieces of dough are resting in a warm place, prepare the topping and heat the oven to its maximum, together with the baking trays.

1/4 cup fenugreek seeds
1 clove garlic
1 cup coriander leaves
1/2 tsp salt
1 tbsp lemon juice
1 fresh green chilli pepper
2 tbsp water

Drain the fenugreek seeds. Put them and all the other ingredients into a blender and mix into a paste. Prick the surface of each pitta bread with a fork, leaving a narrow margin around the edge. Brush the top of each one with a little melted butter or ghee. Spread a teaspoonful of paste over each piece of dough. Place them on the hot baking sheets and cook for no more than 5 minutes. Serve warm.

Yogurt Soup

"The days of our years are threescore years and ten ..." according to the Book of Psalms. Not in the Caucasus they're not. Georgia claims 50 centenarians for every 100,000 inhabitants. One veteran, still riding horses at 117, said he owed it all to a diet rich in vegetables and yogurt and short on meat: short, that is by Georgian standards. Yogurt soups are popular throughout the Middle East. This version is simple, light, distinctive, and delicious. It may or may not make you live to be 100.

---

2 medium onions
2 cups good chicken stock
2 cups yogurt
salt
handful fresh coriander, finely chopped

Sauté the onions in oil until transparent. Bring the chicken stock to a boil. Reduce the heat and add the onion. Simmer for ten minutes. Take the soup off the heat and stir in the yogurt. Reheat the soup but take care not to let the liquid boil, or the yogurt will curdle. Add salt to taste. Stir in a handful of chopped coriander.

Lentil Soup

Lentils have been in cultivation in the Middle East for more than 8,000 years. This modest collection of ingredients, even if combined with water rather than stock, makes a subtle and delicious soup and variations can be found throughout the region.

---

2 cups brown or green lentils
1 onion, chopped
1 stick celery, chopped
1 carrot, peeled, and chopped
1 clove garlic, chopped
1 tsp ground cumin
8 cups water or stock
2 tsp salt, 1 tsp pepper, juice of 1 lemon
3 tbsp butter or vegetable oil

Heat the oil or butter in a large saucepan. Sauté the onion and garlic until soft. Add the celery and carrot and cook for about 5 minutes. Add the lentils and cumin. Stir for 2 minutes. Then add stock or water, bring to a boil, reduce heat and simmer until lentils are cooked (the time varies, but about 30–45 minutes). Liquidize the soup, reheat slowly and season to taste with salt, pepper, and lemon juice. Serve in bowls with a sprinkling of fresh, finely chopped mint.

Kookoo-ye-gol Kalam

Cauliflower Kookoo

The closest relation to the Persian *kookoo* in the European repertoire is the Spanish omelette or *tortilla*. The Persian dish travelled westward with the Arabs and swung north into Spain with the Moors in the eighth century. Both *kookoo* and *tortilla* are deep and firm enough to be cut into wedges and eaten cold. *Kookoo* makes ideal picnic food.

---

1 1/2 cups cauliflower or broccoli
3 tbsp butter, salt and pepper
1 medium onion, chopped
2 cloves garlic, chopped
1 large potato, boiled, skinned, and chopped
1 tbsp self-rising flour
1 tsp turmeric
6 eggs
2 tbsp fresh parsley, finely chopped

Drop the florets into a large saucepan of salted boiling water. Simmer until just tender (about 10 minutes). Drain and mash with a fork. Melt 2 tablespoons butter in a pan. Add the chopped onion, and garlic. Sauté until soft. Combine onion, garlic, cauliflower (or broccoli), potato, flour, and turmeric in a large bowl. Beat the eggs thoroughly, adding the parsley, salt, and pepper. Add this to the rest of the ingredients. Use the rest of the butter to grease a baking dish. Turn the mixture into the dish and bake in an oven preheated to 350°F for about 45 minutes. Serve warm or cold accompanied by a spicy tomato sauce.

Nokhod

Lentils, Chick-peas and Spinach

During the six-hundred-year rule of the Abbasid Caliphs in Baghdad, chick-peas were held in high regard. Amongst many other merits, they were thought to increase the sexual appetite. (Rue had the opposite effect). Whatever the reason, chick-peas remain popular throughout the Middle East, and this dish is a particular favorite of the Kurds.

I cup dried chick-peas
2 tbsp vegetable oil
I cup brown or green lentils
8oz pkg frozen spinach
I large onion, finely chopped
2 cups canned chopped tomatoes
I tbsp chopped fresh dill, or I teaspoon dried dill
salt, pepper, and lemon juice to taste

Soak the chick-peas for 2 or 3 hours. Thaw the spinach. Boil the chick-peas in fresh unsalted water until tender, drain, and set them aside. Fry the onion in a large skillet in the oil until soft. Add the lentils. Stir thoroughly. Add the spinach and tomatoes and enough water just to cover the mixture. Simmer very gently with a lid on for 15 minutes. Add the chick-peas. Simmer for another 15 minutes, until the lentils are cooked. Check regularly to ensure there is enough liquid. Add dill, salt, pepper, and lemon juice to taste.

Imam Bayildi

Stuffed Eggplant

The name of this celebrated dish means "the Imam fainted". Whether he was overcome because of the exquisite flavor or the quantity of costly olive oil will never be known.

---

4 matched eggplant
1 1/2 cups onions, thinly sliced
1 1/2 cups tomatoes, skinned and chopped
3 cloves garlic, finely chopped
2 tbsp parsley, finely chopped
salt, pepper, and the juice of a lemon
1/2 cup olive oil

Cut off the stalk end of the eggplant and keep it as a "plug". Scoop out the flesh with an apple corer but be careful not to break the skin. Sprinkle the inside with salt. Turn the eggplant over to drain the bitter juices drawn out by the salt. Heat three tablespoons of the oil in a pan and soften the onions and garlic very gently until they almost melt. Remove from the heat and stir in the parsley and tomatoes. Season to taste with salt and pepper. Mix thoroughly. Rinse the eggplant under running water and dry with paper towels. Divide the filling equally between the four. Top each one with its plug. Fit them tightly, cap-end upwards, in a tall pan or casserole dish. Add the remaining oil, the lemon juice, and enough water to reach the caps. Cover the pan and bake in the oven, preheated to 375°F for about 1 hour. Serve them hot or cold.

Stuffed Red Peppers

"A table without vegetables is like an old man without wisdom": Arab proverb. Stuffed vegetables and fruit are a central part of the Middle Eastern repertoire of good food. Try this stuffing, or the previous one, in onions, tomatoes, zucchini, potatoes, and apples. Experiment with *burghul* (cracked wheat), chick-peas, chopped vegetables, and dried fruits. A combination of onion, garlic, spinach, and rice is excellent.

---

4 medium red peppers
$1/2$ lb ground lamb
$1/2$ cup long grain rice, washed and drained
1 small onion, finely chopped
1 tomato, skinned and chopped
1 tbsp parsley, finely chopped
$1/2$ tsp ground cinnamon
Stock
salt, tomato purée (optional), pepper, and juice of 1 lemon

Mix all the stuffing ingredients thoroughly and knead so that they bind. Cut the stalk end of each pepper to create a "cap". Remove the seeds and ribs. Stuff each one no more than three-quarters full (the rice will swell). Replace the cap. Stand the peppers in a pan or casserole in which they fit snugly. Add the lemon juice, a teaspoon of salt, half a teaspoon of black pepper, and enough water to cover by an inch. A tablespoon of tomato purée is a good addition. Cover the pan and bake in an oven preheated to 375°F for about one hour, until the peppers are just soft. Serve hot or cold.

Bamia Basrani

Okra with Tomatoes and Onions

Okra, or lady's fingers, a native plant of West Africa, travelled north by caravan across the desert to the Levant, and west to the New World with slaves raided from the Gold Coast and Angola. There it lent its special character to *gumbo*. In the Middle East it is also married with the New World's tomato to make beguiling vegetable, or meat and vegetable, stews.

---

2 cups fresh young okra, or one 14 oz can
3 large tomatoes, skinned and sliced
2 medium onions, thinly sliced
2 cloves of garlic, chopped
5 tbsp olive oil
1 tbsp chopped fresh coriander or 1 tsp ground coriander
salt, pepper, and juice of 1 lemon

To skin the tomatoes, pour boiling water over them and leave to stand for a few moments. The skin can then be peeled away with a sharp knife. If using fresh okra, wash and cut off the stem without cutting into the vegetable itself. If using canned, drain and rinse under running water. Heat the oil in a large pan and sauté the onions and garlic until golden. Add the okra and cook for a few moments stirring gently. Add the tomatoes. Cook for another 2 minutes. Add the coriander, salt and pepper, cover with water, bring to simmering point and cook gently for 30–40 minutes (about half that time if using tinned okra). Stir in the lemon juice and cook for another 15 minutes (5 for canned okra). Serve hot or cold.

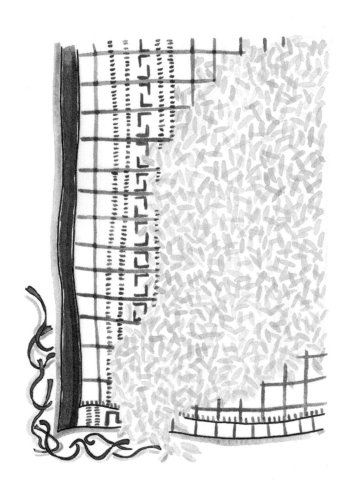

Saffron Rice

In 1935, Freya Stark set off on a donkey with five Bedouin to follow the great frankincense route from the Yemeni coast deep into the Hadhramaut. Lunch was a "mess of rice" mixed with *bisbas* (powdered red pepper) and some of the rotted shark "which makes every caravan in the Hadhramaut smell as if something had died, not very recently, in its midst". Rice came originally from the Indian sub-continent. Alexander the Great may have introduced it when he returned to Babylon in 323 B.C. after defeating the Indian king Poros on the banks of the Indus. At all events, it is the culinary backbone of the Middle East. Every cook has a slightly different method of preparation. Each one is indisputably "the best". This may not be the best but it works.

1/4 cup butter or ghee (clarified butter)
1 cup long grain rice
1 tsp salt tsp powdered saffron or turmeric (optional)
2 1/2 cups boiling water

Wash the rice thoroughly and drain. Melt the butter or ghee in a heavy saucepan, add the rice and fry, stirring constantly, for 2–3 minutes. Add the salt, saffron (or turmeric), and boiling water. Bring back to a boil. After 2 minutes, turn down the heat until just simmering, cover the pan with a tight-fitting lid and leave for about 20 minutes. The liquid should be absorbed, the rice tender. Remove from the heat, fold a clean tea-towel, place over the pan, cover with the lid and leave it for about 15 minutes to retain moisture before serving.

Fish Marinade

Fish cookery in the Middle East tends to be simple in the best sense. It is hard to improve on good fresh fish grilled over charcoal or baked in the oven. The practice of marinating is widespread. These quantities can be no more than a guide. All depends on the size of the fish, whether it is whole, or filleted and cubed for cooking on a kebab stick, the scope of the dish, and above all the preferences of the cook.

---

6 tbsp olive oil
juice of 3 lemons
onion juice to taste (squeeze
small chunks of onion
in a garlic crusher)

fresh basil or tarragon, or bay
leaves, or marjoram,
finely chopped

Mix all ingredients together in a large, shallow dish. Adjust to taste. Then, if using a whole fish, cut two or three incisions on the diagonal across each side of the fish and leave it in the marinade for 2 or 3 hours, turning from time to time.

Sultan Ibrahim Ramleh

Grilled Red Mullet

Sultan Ibrahim Ramleh is the Lebanese name for red mullet. The fish is highly prized in the Eastern Mediterranean and along the north African coast and generally cooked simply – grilled over charcoal or baked. Have the fish market clean and scale it. Marinade it for a couple of hours (see above). Grill it,

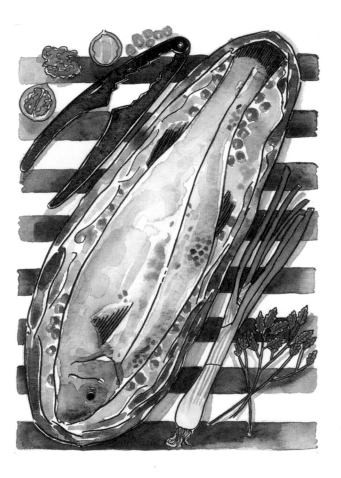

turning the fish once so that both sides become crisp and slightly blistered and the flesh lifts easily away from the bone. Serve with lemon wedges and freshly cooked rice (see p. 35). For a guide to baking, see the recipe for *Samakah Harrah* (see below).

Samakah Harrah

Baked Stuffed Fish

Variations of this dish are found throughout the Arab States, from Alexandria to Baghdad. For special occasions, use a whole bass. Otherwise ask the fish market to recommend any reasonably-priced white fish with firm flesh. The pomegranate is essential; the combination of flavors is exquisite.

---

whole fish weighing up to 4 lbs
1 cup crushed walnuts
1 cup burghul, bulgar or pourgouri (cracked wheat)
2 tbsp spring onion, finely chopped
4 cloves garlic, finely chopped
6 tbsp parsley and coriander, finely chopped and mixed
salt, pepper, and juice of 2 lemons
seeds of one fresh pomegranate

Clean, rinse and dry the fish. Mix all the ingredients, except the pomegranate seeds, in a food processor. Do it quickly to keep the nutty texture, but make it moist enough to bind. Add the pomegranate seeds carefully so as not to crush them. Stuff the fish. Heat the oven to 350°F. Paint a fish-shaped patch with oil onto a sheet of foil. If there is any stuffing left over, put half on the oiled patch. Place the fish on top and the rest of the stuffing on the fish. Make a loose, but tightly-sealed parcel with the foil and bake for about 30–40 minutes. To test, open the parcel, insert a knife and check that the flesh lifts away from the bone.

Patlıçan Koftesi

Eggplant Meatballs

Mediaeval Iraqi physicians recommended eggplant to patients suffering from an obstruction of the kidney or the spleen. This is a Turkish specialty from Ismir.

---

1 lb eggplant, peeled
2 tbsp salt
4–5 tsp vegetable oil
1 large onion, finely chopped
1/2 lb ground lamb
1/4 cup grated hard cheese
2 tbsp chopped parsley
1/2 tsp each oregano, sweet basil, black pepper, salt
seasoned flour, and oil for frying

Cut the eggplant into 1/4 inch slices, sprinkle with salt. Set aside to drain in a colander for 30 minutes then wash under running cold water and pat dry. Heat the oil in a large pan. Cover the bottom of the pan with one layer of eggplant and fry, turning once. Repeat until all the eggplant is fried. Remove when soft and leave on paper towels. Fry the onion until translucent. Place in a medium-size bowl with the meat, cheese, herbs, salt, and

pepper. Chop the eggplant finely, add it to the mixture, knead for 5 minutes. With damp hands, form the mixture into small balls, roll in seasoned flour and chill for 30 minutes. Heat some oil in a large pan, fry the eggplant balls a few at a time for about 15 minutes until cooked through and browned. Serve hot or cold. These are delicious with the walnut dip on page 15.

Mishmishiya

Lamb with Apricots

Members of the leisured classes in mediaeval Baghdad were gourmets by definition. Appreciation of *haute cuisine* – for that's what it was, matched the appreciation of poetry, music, and philosophy in this most cultivated of societies. This subtle combination of lamb, apricots (*mishmish*), and ground almonds comes from the *Kitab al-Tabikh* (Cookery Book) written by Muhammad ibn al-Hassan ibn Muhammad ibn al-Karim al Katib al-Baghdadi in 1226, one of a handful of recipe collections that have survived until today.

1 ¹/₂ cups dried apricots	¹/₂ tsp each ground coriander
1 ¹/₂lb lamb, cut into cubes	and cumin
1 large onion, finely sliced	salt and pepper to taste
3 tbsp olive oil	¹/₂ cup ground almonds
¹/₄ tsp each, ground turmeric,	rose water
cinnamon, and ginger	

Soak the apricots in hot water for an hour. In a large skillet brown the meat in the oil. Add the spices and cook gently for 5 minutes. Season to taste with salt and pepper. Add the onion and the water in which the apricots have soaked. The meat should be just covered, so add more water if necessary. Simmer very gently for half an hour. Stir in the ground almonds. Add the apricots and continue cooking until the meat is just tender. Sprinkle with rose water.

Chicken Chakhokhbili

The fresh herbs give this characteristic Georgian dish its incomparable zestiness. First make the *suneli* (spice mix) by combining in a spice grinder 1 teaspoon each of fenugreek, celery seed, dried basil, mint, thyme, ground coriander, allspice, cinnamon, a pinch of saffron stamens, half a teaspoon each of ground chilli and cumin, and two bay leaves.

1 chicken, cut into serving pieces	*chicken stock or white wine*
2 tbsp butter	*1 tsp paprika*
6 tomatoes, peeled and seeded	*1 tsp turmeric*
1 tsp suneli	*2 tbsp each finely chopped parsley, basil, coriander*
2 large onions, finely chopped	*1 tbsp each chopped mint and tarragon*
6 medium potatoes, boiled and quartered	

In a large skillet, melt half the butter, add the chicken and sauté gently for about 10–15 minutes, pouring off and saving the juices. Set the chicken aside. Melt the remaining butter. Fry the *suneli* for 2–3 minutes, then add the tomatoes, onions, potatoes and

chicken juices. Stir in the turmeric and paprika. Simmer gently for 5 minutes. Add the chicken with either a cup of chicken stock or a glass of white wine. Cover and simmer very gently for about 20–25 minutes. Add the chopped fresh herbs 5 minutes before removing from the heat.

Kirshuh

Liver Stew

This is a simplified version of a dish from the Yemen, where the stew would probably contain a mixture of kidney and heart from either a lamb or a calf.

1 tsp each of turmeric, coriander and cumin, and a scant 1/2 tsp cardamom.	*1 large onion, finely sliced*
	6 tomatoes, skinned and chopped
1 1/2 lb lambs liver	*4 tbsp vegetable oil*
6 cloves garlic	*2 tbsp chopped fresh coriander*
2–3 inch piece of fresh ginger, finely chopped	*salt and pepper to taste*

Dry mix the first 4 ingredients. Add enough water to the spices to make a paste. Cut the liver into bite-size chunks. In a large skillet heat the oil, sauté the onion until soft over a low flame. Add the garlic, then the ginger, stirring each time for 2 or 3 minutes. Add the spice mixture. Cook gently for 2 minutes, still stirring. Then add the liver, raise the flame a little, and cook, stirring constantly, for 5–6 minutes, or until it is brown on the outside and still just pink on the inside. Add the tomatoes, salt, pepper and fresh coriander. Cook for another two or three minutes and then serve with rice (see p. 35).

Mirkatan or Koshab

Dried Fruit Salad

Apricots, raisins, and almonds are essential to the character of this dish, which is found today particularly in Turkey, the Caucasus, and Iran.

---

4 cups dried fruits (apricots,
pears, peaches, prunes, figs)
1 cup blanched almonds
1/2 cup pistachio nuts or pine nuts
1 1/5 cups jasmine, or other delicate tea
1 vanilla bean and half a dozen cardamom seeds
1 pomegranate
2 tbsp brandy (a Caucasian option) or 1 tbsp of rose water

Put all the dried fruits in a bowl, add the nuts, vanilla bean, and cardamom seeds. Cover with the hot, strained tea. When it has cooled, add the brandy or rose water. Leave to macerate overnight at least. The liquid will take on the color of amber. Before serving, scatter the fruit with the seeds of a fresh pomegranate.

Apricot Cream

Many Greek and Asian food shops stock sheets of concentrated apricot pulp-packed in neon-yellow cellophane paper. It is known as *amardine*. The sight revives childhood cravings for packet jelly but this sticky delight creates an altogether more delectable dessert.

1/2 lb packet apricot paste
1 large carton plain yogurt
1/2 cup flaked almonds

Put the sheet of apricot paste in a bowl and cover it with 4 cups of hot water. Leave it to soak for a few hours. Then tip the contents of the bowl into a large pan, bring it slowly to simmering point and continue simmering very slowly, stirring regularly, until the liquid thickens and reduces by about half. Take it off the heat. Let it cool. Stir in the nuts. If you have a very sweet tooth, put it in a serving dish, chill it and serve it with thick cream or *crème fraîche*. To my mind it is even better if you add really good quality plain yogurt (preferably full cream): about one part yogurt to two parts apricot. Chill and serve.

Rutab Mu'assal

Honeyed Dates

Al-Baghdadi, author of the thirteenth century *Kitab al-Tabikh* (Cookery Book) which gives us the recipe for *Mishmishiya* on page 43, claims preeminence for the pleasures of eating, above drink, clothes, sex, scent, and sound. Even the simplest ingredients such as dates – a staple of the rural poor – were transformed into something both refined, beautiful, and hopelessly tempting.

---

2 cups fresh dates
1 cup blanched almonds
2 tbsp honey
3 tbsp rose water
pinch of ground saffron
2 tbsp each icing sugar and ground cinnamon

Make a slit in the side of each date and lift out the stone. Replace it with a blanched almond. Put the honey, rose water and saffron in a small pan, bring to a boil and simmer for 3 minutes. Allow to cool slightly then pour over the dates. Make sure each one is thoroughly coated and leave for a couple of hours. Mix the sugar and cinnamon. Roll each date in the sugar mix.

Soarzeh

Bird's Nest Pastries

In Southern Turkey, these are known as *Anteb bulbulu*, "Anteb nightingale". Listening to the nightingale is some people's idea of heaven. There may be a connection.

---

6 sheets filo or strudel pastry
1/2 cup ghee or clarified butter
1 1/2 cups sugar
1 tbsp lemon juice
1 1/2 cups water
2 tbsp rose water
(makes 36)

Lay the sheets of filo on top of each other. Cut in half lengthwise. Then cut across twice to make 6 equal-size rectangles from each sheet. Stack them and cover with greaseproof paper and a damp cloth to prevent them from drying. Melt the butter. Take one piece of filo, brush the butter over the upper surface. Roll up the filo like a cigarette, bending it into a circle and sticking the ends together with water. Repeat with remaining filo pieces. Heat the oven to 325°F and bake the rings on a baking sheet for 20 minutes, until slightly golden. Meanwhile put the sugar, lemon juice, and water in a pan, bring to a boil and simmer for about 10 minutes. The sugar should be completely dissolved and the liquid slightly thickened. Remove from the heat and stir in the rose water. Take the pastries from the oven, pour the hot syrup over them and leave to cool.

Kunafeh Mounds

You will need a small, round mold, or soup ladle to make these. *Kunafeh* pastry is like fine vermicelli. It's sold frozen in Greek and Levantine delicatessens.

---

2 cups kunafeh *pastry*
1 cup clarified butter or ghee
12 walnut halves
1/2 cup pistachios or
blanched almonds, finely chopped
2 cups sugar
1 1/2 cups water
1 tbsp lemon juice

Pull apart the strands of pastry. Shred it very finely. Mix it thoroughly with most of the melted butter. Take the mold or ladle, coat the inside with melted butter, put a walnut at the bottom, and fill it with pastry. Make a small hole, fill it with finely chopped nuts and cover with more pastry. Press down. Turn it out onto a greased baking tray. Bake the dozen or so mounds in a preheated oven at 350°F for about 40 minutes. Combine the sugar, water, and lemon juice and simmer for 10 minutes. When the pastries are cooked, bring the syrup to a boil and ladle it over them. Allow to cool before serving.

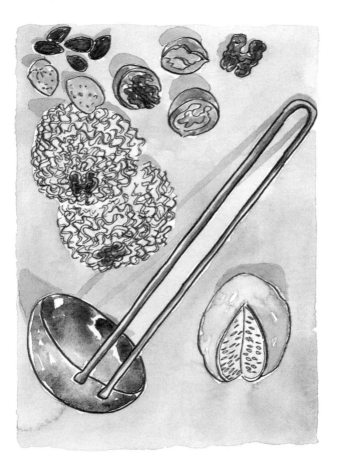

Drinks

Middle Eastern Coffee

The Turks make it in a small copper *ibrik* (*jaswah* in Arabic) although any small flame-proof pot will do.

| 1 tsp sugar (more, or none, to taste) | 1 tsp coffee |
| 1 coffee cup of water |

(serves 1)

Put the sugar and water in the pot. Heat to dissolve the sugar, bring to a boil, remove from heat, add the coffee and bring to a boil again. Remove from the heat until the froth subsides and bring to a boil again. Repeat this twice. Pour straight into a cup. Don't disturb it (because of the sediment). The Armenians add 1 crushed cardamom seed and a drop of orange blossom water. The Anatolians add 2 drops of rose water.

Mint Tea

The quiet cough and grumble of a samovar was, and in some places is, as familiar a background noise in an Iranian, Iraqi, or Kurdish household as in a Russian one. Throughout the region, tea-drinking is a social occasion, even if only two are gathered together. Mint tea and Morocco seem virtually synonymous.

---

3 tsp green tea
handful of fresh whole mint or 1 tbsp dried mint
sugar to taste (optional)

Put the tea in a warmed 6-cup pot, add sugar, and a handful of fresh mint leaves. Pour on boiling water and allow everything to steep for 3 to 4 minutes. Stir and allow to settle.

Index